Contents

INTRODUCTION

Although this material is intended to be used flexibly, we suggest that you begin by working through Units 1 and 2. Unit 1 will help you to identify your own grammatical weaknesses, and indicates which units will help you with specific problem areas. If you decide that you want a general revision course in grammar then you may prefer to work through the complete text.

Unit 2 introduces you to the technical terms which we use in the material. Although we have tried to keep these to a minimum, there are times when it is essential to use them in order to explain a point of grammar. In addition, we feel it is important to understand parts of speech and their functions in sentences. This not only allows you to develop a fuller understanding of your own language but can also assist you when you learn a foreign language.

Before you begin work on the first unit, you will need a sheet of A4 paper or card at the ready to stop yourself reading the answers to Activities before you have written down your own.

UNIT
1

STARTING OUT

Targets

This unit will help you to:

→ consider the importance of grammar;

→ think about the part grammar plays in our speech and writing;

→ decide which units you want to work on.

Although it has always been there in the background, grammar has suddenly become an important subject. It is an essential part of the debate on the National Curriculum and candidates in GCSE exams now lose marks for poor grammar.

What is grammar?

Activity

Consider how you feel about grammar by putting a ✓ or ✗ beside each of the following statements, according to whether you agree with them or not.

When you write, good grammar should be part of good presentation. ☐

Grammar is the backbone of the English language. ☐

Grammar is boring. ☐

Grammar is something people used to learn. ☐

All educated people use grammar correctly. ☐

You can't learn a foreign language unless you understand the grammar of your own. ☐

Grammar is the rules that govern the way language is used. ☐

Good grammar shows you want to make a good impression. ☐

Good grammar helps you to pass exams. ☐

We won't share our views about these statements yet. You'll find out what we think as you work through this unit, and in the Review. It would be best not to look at the Review section until you have worked through the whole unit as you may want to revise some of your ideas in the course of your study.

When is grammar important?

When we speak to friends or family we are usually far too involved in our conversation with them to stop and wonder if our grammar is correct. Anyway, grammar probably doesn't matter here as our friends and family accept us the way we are – warts and all.

It's when we are in formal situations that good grammar is important. We are expected to understand the way the language works and to use the rules correctly.

 ## Activity

> When do you think good grammar is important? Make a list of occasions in the box below. It may help to think of both spoken and written examples.

You may have suggested: writing formal letters, reports, memos, essays, CVs or written exam answers. The spoken occasions might have included interviews and presentations. There are times when we want to create the right impression and we don't want grammatical mistakes to let us down.

Each year in their reports for GCSE, examiners complain about candidates' poor grammar. Many candidates:

■ **don't** write in sentences;

■ **don't** use the correct tense of the verb or use tenses consistently;

■ **use** conversational or slang expressions;

■ **use** clichés (over-worked phrases) instead of a varied vocabulary.

Faulty grammar can lead examiners to believe that your knowledge and understanding of a subject are not sufficient. Poor grammar can prevent you from communicating your knowledge and understanding accurately.

Activity

Since such a high priority seems to be placed on grammar in exams and formal writing tasks, what does good grammar do for our writing? Note your suggestions below.

You could have mentioned that good grammar helps you to ensure that:

■ your message is accurate and unambiguous – you end up writing what you want to say;

■ you express yourself as concisely as possible.

By the way

We would also suggest the following reasons for learning about grammar:

■ A knowledge of grammar helps you to understand the structure of the language.

■ Knowing how to use grammar correctly gives you the confidence to know that you can write and speak correctly for formal occasions.

■ The use of good grammar shows your reader or listener that you know what is acceptable in standard English – it creates the right impression.

■ Knowing about the grammar of, and the grammatical terms used in, your own language helps when you come to learn a foreign language.

Which grammar points do you need to work on?

It may be that you are already aware of some of the points you need to work on. However, if you find it hard to identify these, you could:

■ do a piece of writing for your tutor and ask him or her to point out any grammatical errors and comment upon your grammar in general;

■ look through past pieces of work and note down any criticisms of your grammar;

■ look at the targets at the beginning of each unit in this book and decide if you need any advice on the points covered.

Activity

You can also decide which units to study by looking at the following passage and underlining words and phrases that you feel need changing. When you have finished, try to write a corrected version.

The journey from Norfolk should have took two hours but as it was Friday it takes three and a half hours so I was not up to having an argument. In addition to this I had also left Norfolk slightly later than planned as Brett, my mate, lent my car. He wanted to take his mother to the station. It would be dark now when I arrived.

I knew I should have contacted Nasreen before but I had been very busy lately. She would be concerned when I arrived without having telephoned her first. She would look at me reproachfully and say, 'I've been worried about you. Why can't you never phone?' It was always the same: her dark eyes would make me feel guilty and I would vow never ever to lie to her again.

I have known Nasreen for three years now. We was in the same group at college. She was by far the best student in the class; I was the worse. She and me were like peas in a pod. We had the same interests and liked the same people. Booze and sport had occupied most of my time until then but slowly Nasreen changed my way of life. At school I always missing lessons but at college I attended every session so that I could be with Nasreen. I also liked Anne, our lecturer. She always said that knowing her had been a good influence on me.

You should have underlined the following: should have took; it takes three; up to having; I had also; my mate; lent my car; I should of; can't you never; never ever; we was; was the worse; she and me; like peas in a pod; booze; knowing her.

Here is a corrected version:

The journey from Norfolk should have taken two hours but as it was Friday it took three and a half hours so I was not prepared for an argument. In addition to this I had left Norfolk slightly later than planned as Brett, my friend, had borrowed my car. He wanted to take his mother to the station. It would be dark now when I arrived.

I knew I should have contacted Nasreen before but I had been very busy lately. She would be concerned when I arrived without having telephoned her first. She would look at me reproachfully and say, 'I've been worried about you. Why can't you ever phone?' It was always the same: her dark eyes would make me feel guilty and I would vow never to lie to her again.

I have known Nasreen for three years now. We were in the same group at college. She was by far the best student in the class; I was the worst. She and I were very alike. We had the same interests and liked the same people. Drink and sport had occupied most of my time until then but slowly Nasreen changed my way of life. At school I was always missing lessons but at college I attended every session so that I could be with Nasreen. I also liked Anne, our lecturer. She always said that knowing Nasreen had been a good influence on me.

You may have realised that you sometimes make similar errors. If that is the case, you may want to study a particular unit in which that error is dealt with so that you can understand why what you are doing is wrong and find out how to put it right. In the version of the passage below, you will see that you are signposted to the units which deal with those particular problems.

Unit 7
changing tense

Unit 3
colloquialism

Unit 5
incorrect choice of verb

Unit 6
subject/verb agreement

Unit 6
object instead of subject pronoun

Unit 3
use of over-worked simile

The journey from Norfolk should have <u>took</u> two hours but as it was Friday it <u>takes</u> three and a half hours so I was not <u>up to having</u> an argument. In addition to this I had <u>also left</u> Norfolk slightly later than planned as Brett, my <u>mate</u>, <u>lent</u> my car. He wanted to take his mother to the station. It would be dark now when I arrived.

I knew I should have contacted Nasreen before but I have been very busy lately. She <u>would be</u> concerned when I arrived without having telephoned her first. She would look at me reproachfully and say, 'I've been worried about you. Why can't you <u>never</u> phone?' It was always the same: her dark eyes would make me feel guilty and I would vow never <u>ever</u> to lie to her again.

I have known Nasreen for three years now. We <u>was</u> in the same group at college. She was by far the best student in the class; I was the <u>worse</u>. She and <u>me</u> were like <u>peas in a pod</u>. We had the same interests and liked the same people. <u>Booze</u> and sport had occupied most of my time until then but slowly Nasreen changed my way of life. At school I was always missing lessons but at college I attended every session so that I could be with Nasreen. I also liked Anne, <u>our</u> lecturer. She always said that knowing <u>her</u> had been a good influence on me.

Unit 7
incorrect past participle

Unit 3
colloquialism

Unit 3
tautology

Unit 4
double negative

Unit 3
tautology

Unit 5
comparatives and superlatives

Unit 3
slang

Unit 4
ambiguous pronoun

Review

At the beginning of this unit we said that we would summarise our views on grammar here so that you could check your responses to the first activity in this unit. Here they are:

- Grammar is indeed the backbone of the English language: the rules that govern the way the language is used.

- People still learn grammar. It isn't a thing of the past and it need not be boring if it is presented in the right way and you can see the relevance of it.

- Correct grammar is part of good presentation. It creates the right image, which will contribute towards passing exams.

- Knowing the grammar of your own language will certainly be useful when you learn another language.

UNIT 2

BACKGROUND INFORMATION

Targets

This unit will help you to:

→ understand what we mean when we refer to 'parts of speech';

→ become familiar with verbs, their tenses and forms;

→ follow more easily the suggestions we make in other units.

Before you can learn about any subject, you need to understand its background. In this unit you will be developing your understanding of English grammar by looking at the technical words used to describe it. There is no need to try to learn everything in this unit in one sitting. We suggest you work through it once, tackling the activities as you go, and then return to it for reference as you encounter technical words in later units.

We now want you to consider what role the various parts of speech play within sentences. We'll give you several examples of each part of speech within a sentence or sentences and then ask you to work out the function of the part of speech. You will probably need to study the sentences carefully. When you have noted down your ideas, you will be able to check them against ours.

Nouns

Activity

Read the following passage. All the nouns in it have been highlighted.

Nina and **Pip** went shopping in **Bristol** last **Saturday**. They bought several **items** for their new **home** including a **cooker**, a **microwave**, a **table** and three **cushions**.

Now try to complete this sentence describing the function of a noun:

A noun can refer to

You probably noticed that the nouns referred to

people	a day	places	objects
Nina Pip	Saturday	Bristol home	items cooker microwave table cushions

Adjectives

Activity

In the next passage the adjectives have been highlighted. Can you work out what an adjective does? You may find it helpful to look at the words which follow the adjectives.

> Winter has us in its **icy** hold. **Each** morning when we wake we see **white** lawns, **long**, **spiky** icicles and **brilliant blue** skies.

> An adjective

'Hold, morning, lawns, icicles and skies' are all nouns. As you can see, the adjectives give more information about the nouns.

Pronouns

Activity

All the pronouns in the passage below have been highlighted. Before you complete the statement about pronouns, you may like to concentrate on **they** and **he** and work out which words these have replaced.

> The children ran into the room. **They** were all trying to talk at once. Ron managed to make **himself** heard. **He** said, '**Everyone** has been invited to dinner.'

> A pronoun

If you found it difficult to work out what function the pronouns are performing in the sentences, study this:

> The children ran into the room. **The children** were all trying to talk at once. Ron managed to make **Ron** heard. **Ron** said, '**The family** has been invited to dinner.'

You will see that the words 'they', 'himself', 'he', 'everyone' have replaced some of the nouns. A pronoun is used instead of a noun to produce more flowing and less repetitive sentences.

Verbs

Activity

All the verbs in the following sentences have been highlighted. You will notice that sometimes the verb consists of one word and sometimes of several words.

Read the passage and then try to complete the sentence about verbs.

> The swimming pool **was** busy. Some people **were swimming** up and down the pool. Others **were queueing** for the diving board. As each person **reached** the front of the queue he or she **looked** down into the clear water, **stretched** and then **jumped**.

> A verb

You will probably have found it easy to work out that the words 'were swimming', 'looked', 'jumped' and others show us which actions are being performed. A verbs tells us which actions are happening within a sentence. Two verbs, 'to be' and 'to have', are more difficult to recognise. Look again at the first sentence of the passage: 'The swimming pool was busy.' 'Was' is a form of the verb 'to be'. Other examples of these two verbs are:

We had a super time. (from the verb 'to have')

I am disappointed. (from the verb 'to be')

You will be finding out more about verbs later in this unit and in Unit 7.

Adverbs

If you think about the word **adverb**, it may give you a clue as to the part an adverb plays in a sentence.

Activity

Look at the examples of adverbs highlighted in the sentences below and then complete the sentence that follows.

> Tim ran **hurriedly** into the garden. The rain was beginning to soak his washing. He **hastily** unpegged the sheets and towels and then, picking up the washing basket, he turned and **quickly** rushed back into the house.

> An adverb

You will probably have seen that the adverbs 'hurriedly', 'hastily' and 'quickly' told us how the actions of running, unpegging and rushing were performed. An adverb usually describes how, where or when an action is carried out.

Prepositions

Activity

> The prepositions have been highlighted in this passage.
>
> > Raffles was finally found snuggled **in** Mike's bed **with** the water bottle. Dirty paw-prints showed that the cat had been **under** the settee, **on** the table, and **inside** the wardrobe.
>
> See if you can finish this sentence. Look at the nouns which follow the prepositions.
>
> > A preposition shows

You might have seen that the prepositions 'in', 'under', 'on', and 'inside', showed a relationship between the cat and the:

■ water bottle – it was **with** the water bottle

■ bed – it was **in** the bed

■ settee – it had been **under** the settee

■ table – it had been **on** the table

■ wardrobe – it had been **inside** the wardrobe.

A preposition shows a relationship between a noun or pronoun and some other word in the sentence.

More about verbs

We look at verbs in more detail in the following units:

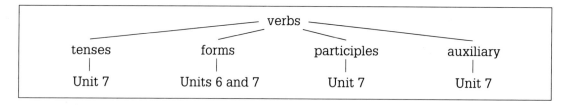

	verbs		
tenses	forms	participles	auxiliary
Unit 7	Units 6 and 7	Unit 7	Unit 7

However, the terms we use in those units are explained here.

Tenses

There are three main verb tenses:

■ past tense – Sue was very happy with her present.

■ present tense – John hates sport.

■ future tense – We will see you on Sunday.

> > or (less frequently but equally correct):
>
> > We shall see you on Sunday.

When we refer to the tense of a verb, we're really talking about the time when an action is happening and that may be in the past, present or future. Some further tenses are formed by one main verb, for example:

■ present simple – He runs.

■ past simple – She sang.

Auxiliary verbs

Other tenses need an additional verb, referred to as an auxiliary verb, for example:

■ present continuous – I am thinking
                              |
                        auxiliary verb

■ past continuous – Gomez was eating
                              |
                        auxiliary verb

■ past perfect – I had written
                        |
                 auxiliary verb.

By the way

The original verb in these three cases (**thinking**, **eating**, **written**) is described as being the 'participle' or 'in the participle form'.

 ## Activity

Can you complete the following sentence about auxiliary verbs?

> An auxiliary verb helps to show

We would have used these words: 'the time when an action is happening'.

Infinitives

The infinitive form of a verb is simply the verb as it appears when preceded by **to**. These verbs are shown in the infinitive:

to sleep to push to wonder.

An infinitive doesn't show:

- who is carrying out the action;
- when the action is happening.

Activity

Check your understanding of what we have covered so far in this section by underlining the auxiliary verbs and the infinitives in the sentence below. Can you also work out which tense the sentence is written in?

> I was hoping to go to Russia last year, but Tony told me that he had decided to visit Italy and I agreed to travel with him.

You will have seen that the auxiliary verbs are: was (**was** hoping) and had (**had** decided); the infinitives are: to go, to visit, to travel. The sentence is written in the past tense.

Irregular verbs

When we talk about verbs being regular or irregular, we are referring to whether the verbs follow the regular or usual pattern of forms for that tense.

Look at how we form these verbs in the present simple tense:

Singular – one person involved in the action

	to move	**to be**
1st person	I move	I am
2nd person	you move	you are
3rd person	he moves, she moves, it moves	he is, she is, it is

Plural – more than one person involved in the action

	to move	**to be**
1st person	we move	we are
2nd person	you move	you are
3rd person	they move	they are

Activity

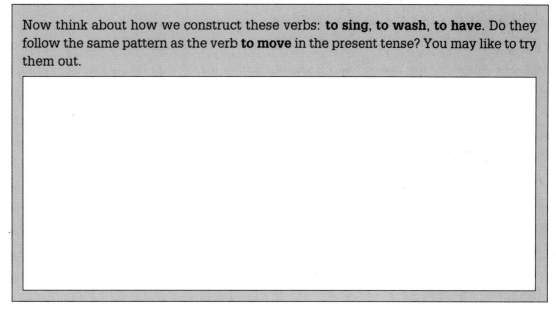

Now think about how we construct these verbs: **to sing**, **to wash**, **to have**. Do they follow the same pattern as the verb **to move** in the present tense? You may like to try them out.

'To sing' and 'to wash' follow the same pattern as 'to move': they are regular verbs. 'To have' doesn't follow the pattern (have, have, has, have, have, have). It is an irregular verb. The verb 'to be' is also an irregular verb.

Regular verbs	Irregular verbs
An **s** or **t** is added to the 3rd person singular of regular verbs in the present simple tense. All the other verb forms are alike.	There are no rules. We have to learn the pattern of each irregular verb.

In the past simple tense, regular verbs end in **ed**.

I moved	you moved	he moved	we moved	you moved	they moved
I was	you were	he was	we were	you were	they were

So the verb **to be** is also irregular in the past simple tense.

Review

You should now feel able to answer 'yes' to each of these questions:

- Do you understand what nouns, adjectives, pronouns, verbs, adverbs and prepositions are?

- Do you have a clearer idea about verb forms and tenses?

- Do you feel you have sufficient background information to feel confident about moving on to other units?

If you answered 'no' to one or more of these questions, check back to the relevant part of this unit.

UNIT
3

PITFALLS

Targets

This unit will help you to:

→ identify words and phrases which you should avoid;

→ explain why they shouldn't be used;

→ replace such words and phrases with more acceptable alternatives.

When we refer to 'good grammar' in this book, we are thinking of the grammar you need for formal writing tasks and the formal occasions when your speech needs to be grammatically correct. We are not trying to influence the way you normally speak. The diagram below shows some of the pitfalls you will need to avoid if you want to practise good grammar.

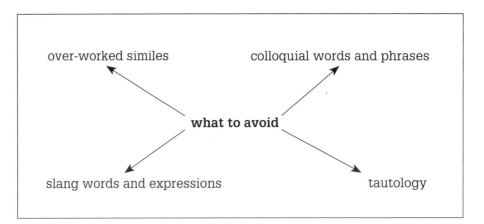

over-worked similes   colloquial words and phrases

what to avoid

slang words and expressions   tautology

Activity

Some of the phrases and words in the diagram will be familiar to you, others will not. We suggest you write down the meaning of those you know in the box below; then use your dictionary to check them and fill in the others.

colloquialism:

(continued opposite)

simile:
tautology:
slang:

Most people's speech has a fair sprinkling of all of these – you are probably aware of using them yourself.

Colloquialisms

A colloquial word or phrase is one that is used in everyday conversation. Colloquialisms are fine for familiar situations, but you should avoid them in formal situations.

Activity

See if you can underline the colloquial words and phrases in this letter to a customer.

> Johnsons Wholesalers Limited
> Hurst Street
> Brighton
> East Sussex BN7 4BP
>
> Fulton & Stroud
> Clifton Buildings
> Evesham
> Worcs WR3 2RT
>
> May 23rd 1993
>
> Dear Mrs Fulton
>
> We are sorry that the latest consignment of umbrellas did not come up to the mark. Obviously any gaffe we make puts us on the spot and the whole work force is under a cloud. The only excuse we can offer is that we have been up against it recently.
>
> We fully appreciate that you were livid when you received your order and that if we are unable to rectify the situation immediately your business will be clobbered. Johnsons values you as a customer and is putting its best foot forward to make amends and we can assure you that another consignment of umbrellas will wing their way to you today.
>
> Please do not hesitate to give us a buzz if you have any further difficulties.
>
> Yours sincerely
>
> *Robert Simpson*
> Robert Simpson

You probably underlined the following: come up to the mark; gaffe, puts us on the spot; under a cloud; up against it; livid; clobbered; putting its best foot forward; give us a buzz.

If such a letter had been sent to a customer it would have created the wrong impression and Johnsons may have lost a customer.

Activity

> Rewrite the letter by replacing each of the colloquial phrases with a more formal and exact one. This is also an opportunity for you to practise your skills at writing a formal letter. Use a separate sheet for your draft.

Here are our ideas. You may have chosen a slightly different way of replacing the phrases. This doesn't matter as long as you haven't altered the meaning of the letter and as long as it has a formal tone.

```
Dear Mrs Fulton

We are sorry that the latest consignment of umbrellas was unsatisfactory.
Obviously any mistake we make embarrasses us and the whole work force is under
suspicion. The only excuse we can offer is that we have been extremely busy
recently.

We fully appreciate that you were very angry when you received your order and
that if we are unable to rectify the situation immediately your business will
be in serious difficulties. Johnsons values you as a customer and is doing
everything possible to make amends and we can assure you that another
consignment of umbrellas will be despatched to you today.

Please do not hesitate to telephone/contact us if you have any further
difficulties.
```

Activity

> Here are some further conversational phrases you should avoid in more formal writing. Underline each and then by the side write a more formal way of expressing it. The first is done for you.
>
> ■ He is always <u>humming and hawing</u>. | dithering |
>
> ■ The family has experienced its ups and downs. | |
>
> ■ I have warned him time and time again. | |
>
> ■ I have looked high and low for it. | |
>
> ■ There are no hard and fast rules for doing this. | |

The underlined phrases should be: ups and downs; time and time again; high and low; hard and fast. Our suggestions for replacing these with more formal words are: problems; repeatedly; everywhere; definite.

Over-worked similes

A simile is a comparison. It compares an object or a person with something else. Here are four examples:

■ Phillip is **as crafty as a fox**.

■ Angela admired Maria who was as **agile as a monkey**.

■ The water in the swimming pool is **like ice**.

■ As she relaxed in the hospital bed, Ursula's face was **as white as a sheet**.

You'll see that the words **as** or **like** always appear in a simile.

By comparing Ursula's face to a sheet, we hope to show just how white her face was. Such expressions are so well known to us that they cease to be descriptive and no longer make an impact. We know what is coming next.

Activity

Here are some further similes for you to complete:

The tyre was as flat as a

Our dog is now as blind as a

The point was as sharp as a

His whole body trembled like a

She will soon be as right as

You probably chose the following comparisons: pancake, bat, needle or razor, leaf, rain.

Although you should avoid using over-familiar similes in formal writing and speech, original carefully constructed similes can be very effective. They can add colour and clarity to your writing.

By the way

Metaphors are like similes in that they make comparisons, but they do not use the words **as** or **like**. In the following examples the metaphors are highlighted.

■ The small boy **snaked** his way up the steeply sloping street, expertly dodging the tourists who ambled in the warm sunshine.

■ Gerd was always a **busy bee**.

■ The mechanic listened to the **purr** of the engine and congratulated herself on her morning's work.

■ Mrs Hill held her in an **iron** grip as she struggled in vain to free herself.

Original metaphors can enhance your descriptive or narrative writing but others are overworked and are best avoided, for example, 'busy bee'; 'purr' (of the engine); 'iron grip'.

Tautology

Tautology occurs when you needlessly repeat an idea you have already expressed.

Activity

See if you can spot the unnecessary repetition in this passage:

> Chris sat alone on his own at the table. He held the unique, triangular paper weight, the only one of its kind, gently in his hand. As he looked into its milky depths, he could see a red tongue of flame protruding out of the apex. He knew he would have to return the treasure back to its owner later; for the moment he regarded it as his own.
>
> The waiter approached for payment. Chris knew that when he had paid his bill it would leave him with only £1.50 left. If only he could substitute a fake paper weight in its place, he would have all the money he needed.

As Chris was on his own, 'alone' isn't needed. Unique means 'the only one of its kind' so it can stand alone. 'Out' isn't needed with 'protrude' which means 'to stick out'. Return means 'to give back' so 'back' after treasure should be omitted. You don't need 'left' after £1.50 as 'leave' has already expressed this idea. In the last line 'in its place' is unnecessary as 'substitute' means 'to put in place of another'.

It is all too easy to become so involved in what you are writing that you mistakenly repeat ideas. Always check your writing when you have completed it so that you can prune any unnecessary words or phrases.

Slang

Slang words are used in informal speech but are unacceptable for formal occasions. Unlike colloquialisms, slang words are usually intended to be in some way irreverent. If you are uncertain whether a word is considered to be slang, you can always check in your dictionary. Probably one of the best-known forms of slang is Cockney Rhyming Slang, for example:

whistle and flute – suit   **skin and blister** – sister   **April showers** – flowers.

Activity

Each of these words can be considered to be slang when used in a certain way. Can you write the acceptable word you would use in its place?

1 in the **nick**		2 a **fag**	
3 to **peg out**		4 **cheesed off**	
5 **nifty**		6 **take the mickey**	
7 **give some stick**		8 **knackered**	
9 **grotty**		10 **yucky/yukky**	

You could have chosen: (1) prison; (2) cigarette; (3) die; (4) disgruntled; (5) smart or quick; (6) mock, tease or annoy; (7) punish; (8) exhausted; (9) useless or in bad condition; (10) dirty, unpleasant.

Review

By now you are aware of some of the informal, chatty words and expressions to avoid in your formal speech and writing:

■ expressions which don't add meaning to what you are saying, for example **to tell you the truth**;

■ words and phrases that everyone uses for example. 'You will never **get to the top**';

■ slang words and phrases, for example 'Let's take a **butcher's** at him';

■ words and phrases that repeat what you've already said for example 'This vase is **equally** as valuable as the one in the window'.

You can avoid such mistakes by:

■ being aware that they are unacceptable;

■ developing a wider vocabulary so that you do not need to resort to them;

■ reading widely so that you can see how other people express their ideas;

■ checking your work carefully to make certain you have not used such words and phrases.

BEING PRECISE

Targets

This unit will help you to:

→ understand the importance of being precise;

→ recognise the occasions when your speech and writing could be ambiguous;

→ be more exact in your speaking and writing.

In this unit we look at some examples of imprecise or ambiguous writing – those occasions when the writer fails to 'get the point across'.

Activity

Can you spot how the writers of the following sentences have failed to express their ideas clearly? Underline the words that you think are the cause of the problem in each case.

1 I can't find no one to clean my windows.

2 I put the book on the table with the damaged cover.

3 The boy lent his friend his car which he crashed.

In (1) the writer has used a double negative; in (2) the words 'with the damaged cover' seem to refer to the table, but common sense tells us that it must be the book's cover that is damaged; in (3) we are left uncertain about who crashed the car.

The rest of this unit tackles each of these problems in turn. The sections which cover these points are:

■ *Being positive* – (1)

■ *Out of order* – (2)

■ *A certain person* – (3).

Being positive

You have already seen that the sentence 'I can't find no one to clean my windows' contains two negatives:

■ can't, that is cannot;

■ no one.

Two negative words within the same sentence can create the opposite effect to the one the writer is trying to convey: they cancel each other out. If a person 'can't find no one' he or she must be able to find someone. So the first sentence in the previous activity should read: 'I can't find **anyone** to clean my windows.'

By the way

Sometimes it is permissible to use 'No' and another negative in a sentence:

No, I don't know where he is.

This is because the speaker is answering a question with 'No' and then expanding the answer.

Activity

Read the following sentences and decide whether they make sense. If you decide the sentence doesn't make sense, try to alter it so that the message is clearer.

1 There wasn't no one in the room.

2 Neither Tim nor Tina wasn't there.

3 Rosario isn't nowhere in sight.

4 No, none of the employees has gone home.

5 Nobody can't lift that weight.

In each of (1), (2), (3), and (5) one of the negative words needs to be changed. These are our suggestions : (1) There wasn't anyone in the room; (2) Neither Tim nor Tina was there; (3) Rosario is nowhere in sight *or* Rosario isn't anywhere in sight. Sentence (5) could be: Nobody can lift that weight.

Out of order

Look back to page 24. In the sentence 'I put the book on the table with the damaged cover', the phrase 'with the damaged cover' should have been placed nearer to the word it describes, that is, the book.

This sentence would be clearer as:

> I put the book with the damaged cover on the table.

 ## Activity

Think about why each of the following sentences may be confusing and then try to express the idea more clearly.

1   Pat sent a letter to the company on her fax machine.

2   She sold the cake to the customer with blue icing.

3   The house is situated near the station with a large front garden.

4   Peter looked for the book in the cupboard that belongs to Sally.

5   By displaying the reduced price of the house, the agent tried to attract buyers in the window.

You will have noticed that in each sentence a phrase has been placed at the end and not next to the word it refers to, making it less clear what the writer means. It would have been clearer to write:

1   Pat sent a letter on her fax machine to the company.

2   She sold the cake with blue icing to the customer.

3   The house with a large front garden is situated near the station.

4   Peter looked in the cupboard for the book that belongs to Sally.

5   By displaying in the window the reduced price of the house, the agent hoped to attract buyers.

You may be able to identify a similar reason for doubt about the meaning of this sentence:

> Being over 1000m, she was determined to climb the mountain.

The impression given is that the climber is over 1000m, not the mountain!

A certain person

Pronouns can sometimes cause confusion.

In the sentence 'The boy lent his friend his car which he crashed' (page 24), we imagine that the boy's friend crashed the car, but because the pronouns 'he' and 'his' have been used so much we can end up feeling uncertain.

Activity

Read the passage below and then answer the questions that follow.

> The college wants students to take more care of their property. A spokeswoman said today that she was sure that, in the main, they were careful but certain elements were abusing the facilities they provided. These facilities were paid for by local residents and they would be appalled by the damage caused by some of them recently.

■ Whose property should students take more care of?

■ Who is providing the facilities?

■ Who caused the recent damage?

You may well have hesitated before giving your answers. The pronouns **they** and **them** could refer to either the college, the students or the residents. The passage is ambiguous.

Activity

Now rewrite the passage above so that it is clearer. You should try to replace some of the confusing pronouns with suitable nouns.

Here is one possible rewrite:

> The college wants students to take more care of the college's property. A spokeswoman said today that she was sure that, in the main, the students were careful but certain elements were abusing the facilities the college provided. These facilities were paid for by local residents who would be appalled by the damage caused by some of the students recently.

You may feel that by replacing the pronouns with nouns we have made the meaning clearer, but that the passage has become rather repetitive (the word 'college' has been used three times). You may prefer to alter the passage more drastically so that you avoid this repetition.

Review

In this unit you have seen why it is necessary to use words with care in order to get your message across as clearly as possible. In future, when you review your writing, check that you have avoided:

- double meanings;
- phrases in the wrong place;
- ambiguous pronouns.

UNIT 5

CHOOSING THE RIGHT WORD

Targets

This unit will help you to:

➜ identify pairs of words that can cause confusion;

➜ make the right choice of word to convey your meaning.

Which verb do you need?

We're now going to look at three pairs of verbs that you may find troublesome.

Lend:borrow

Lend

The verb **to lend** means 'to allow (someone) to have temporary use of (something)':

I will **lend** you my magnifying glass.

The verb forms are: **lend, lends, lent, lending**.

Borrow

The verb **to borrow** means 'to obtain on loan or trust':

Jason would like to **borrow** my car.

The verb forms are: **borrow, borrows, borrowing, borrowed**.

Activity

You can practise using these verbs by correcting the mistakes in the following conversation. We have changed the first one for you as a guide.

Lynn: ~~Borrow~~ *lend* me your calculator, Francis.

Francis: You can lend it for this session.

Lynn: I'm always having to lend your things. Sorry!

Francis: It doesn't matter. I've lent my sister's calculator today.

Lynn: Is she good about borrowing you things?

Francis: No, but I make her because I'm always lending her my videos.

You probably made the following corrections: 'You can borrow it…'; '..having to borrow…'; 'I've borrowed my sister's…'; 'about lending you…'.

Lie:lay

The verb **to lie** has two meanings:

'to rest in a flat position' verb forms: **lie, lies, lying, lay, lain** I **lie** in bed and read. She **lies** there every day. I am **lying** on the sofa. On Saturday he **lay** in bed until 11a.m. Cliff has **lain** there for 30 minutes.	'to say something which is untrue' verb forms: **lie, lies, lying, lied** I **lie** occasionally. She always **lies**. Ray knew John was **lying**. Russell **lied** to me.

The verb **to lay** means: 'to put something on a surface' or 'to produce (eggs)'

> verb forms: **lay, lays, laying, laid**.
>
> I always **lay** the table each morning.
>
> Ian **lays** his book on the shelf.
>
> The hen **laid** three eggs this morning.
>
> Mr Coe knew Robin had **laid** the tiles.
>
> She is **laying** an egg especially for you.

By the way

You can increase your chances of choosing the right alternative if you remember that:

- You always have to lay **something**, for example an egg or table, or place **something** on **something** else, for example, **lay** a blanket on the grass.

- **Lay** is used as the past tense of the verb **to lie** (to rest in a flat position). 'Yesterday I lay on the sofa.'

- **Layed** is not a word: the past tense or past participle of **lay** is **laid**.

Activity

Check your knowledge of **lie** and **lay** by completing this passage:

Daniel viewed the foundations that the builder had ☐ that morning. He knew Joe Benson had been ☐ when he had insisted that the ground had been excavated to a depth of 1.5 metres. Tomorrow morning he would not ☐ in bed until 9.30 as he usually did every Saturday but be up by seven o'clock to confront Joe.

On Saturday morning Daniel paced up and down the kitchen. By 8.30 he was angry, having ☐ in wait for Joe for one and a half hours. He dialled Joe's number. As soon as Joe answered, Daniel shouted, 'I will ☐ my cards on the table. If you don't come round here immediately, I will find another builder.'

You should have chosen: laid, lying, lie, lain, lay.

Infer:imply

Infer means 'to conclude' or 'to deduce' (from the facts given).

Imply means 'to hint' or 'to express indirectly'.

	Infer	**Imply**
verb parts:	infer, infers, inferring, inferred	imply, implies, implying, implied
noun:	inference	implication

Examples include:

- She **implied** that I had deceived her.

- Having listened to Joel's rambling explanation, Ann **inferred** that she was not wanted at the meeting.

By the way

Note the spelling of:

- **inferring**, **inferred**: A double **r** is needed in both of these, whereas **infer**, **infers**, **inference** each has only one **r**;

- **imply**, **implying**: These have a **y** whereas in **implies**, **implied**, **implication** the **y** is replaced by **i**.

Activity

> Note which verb is needed in each of the following sentences.
>
> - As I listened to their conversation I [   ] that they always disagreed about financial matters.
>
> - Graham tried to [   ] to his secretary that he wasn't interested in promotion.
>
> - I did not mean to [   ] that you were lying.
>
> - Despite your reassurances I can only [   ] that you will no longer need to use our company's services.

The correct choices were: inferred; imply; imply; infer.

Making choices

Former:latter

Latter means 'later' and is used to refer to the last-mentioned or 'later' of two alternatives. **Former** means 'the first-mentioned of two choices' or the 'earlier' of two alternatives.

Here are two examples:

I have studied both Spanish and Hindi; the **former** is my specialism.   (the first)

Last year I went to Greece and Malta; I enjoyed the **latter** more.   (the last)

- ■ **Former** can be used only to refer to two options.

- ■ **Latter** is also used for two choices although it can also be used in expressions such as '*In the latter part* of his career he was less conscientious.'

Activity

> Use **former** or **latter** to replace the highlighted word in each sentence below.
>
> Kelly and Leon are both very knowledgeable on the subject but **Leon** explains things more clearly.
>
> He always makes a rich fruit cake or a gateau for weekends; I prefer the **gateau**.
>
> My **previous** boss was so impatient.
>
> Sue is always busy in the **last** part of the financial year.

You should have chosen; (the) latter, the latter, former, latter.

Beside:besides

Activity

> Each of the following words or phrases can be replaced by either **beside** or **besides**. See if you can decide which in each case.
>
> | | beside | besides |
> | --- | --- | --- |
> | 1 next to | | |
> | 2 in addition to | | |
> | 3 near | | |
> | 4 to the side | | |
> | 5 moreover | | |
> | 6 by the side of | | |
> | 7 other than | | |

Definitions (1), (3), (4) and (6) go with **beside**; (2), (5) and (7) describe **besides**.

By the way

Beside is also used in the colloquial expressions:

■ **beside oneself,** meaning very angry or losing self-control;

■ **beside the point,** meaning irrelevant.

Better:best, worse:worst

Activity

See if you can work out rules for the use of these adjectives by looking at the following sets of examples. Write in your rules in the spaces below the examples.

■ Crumpton's brand is a **better** buy than Lipton's but Chamber's is **best**.

■ I feel **better** than I did yesterday.

■ It's the **best** I've felt for a week.

■ Minorca is **better** than Majorca as it is less crowded but Ibiza is the **best** of the Balearic Islands.

■ Although I did **better** in maths than physics, biology was my **best** result.

Rule for better:best

The fog was worse than last night: it was the worst journey I have had since I started travelling to London. The worst section is on the motorway where there are so many fast vehicles. Unfortunately the fog lights on my new car are worse than those on my Escort.

Rule for worse:worst

'Better' is used when making a comparison between two items, whereas 'best' is used if there are three or more items. We use 'worse' when we compare two items and 'worst' for three or more.

By the way

Better and **best** are related to the adjective **good**. **Good** is called the positive form; **better** the comparative form and **best** the superlative form.

good	better	best
one item or person	two items or persons	three or more items or persons
positive	*comparative*	*superlative*

Worse and **worst** are related to the adjective **bad**. **Bad** is the positive; **worse** is the comparative and **worst** is the superlative.

bad	worse	worst
one item or person	two items or persons	three or more items or persons
positive	*comparative*	*superlative*

More:most

More is used to compare two items. It is the comparative form of the adjective **much**. **Most** is the superlative form used to compare three or more items. Here are two examples:

- I collected **more** money today than yesterday. (comparing two days)
- Of Lucille's six friends, she earns the **most**. (comparing six friends)

Less:least

Less and **least** follow a similar pattern to **more** and **most**.

Less is the comparative form of the adjective **little**; it is used to compare two items. **Least** is the superlative form dealing with three or more items in a comparison. For example:

- Misha has **less** enthusiasm than she had last term. (comparing two terms)
- Wayne was the **least** athletic of their three children. (comparing three children)

Many:fewer; much:less

These two pairs of words can sometimes be confused. To distinguish between the two pairs remember that:

Many and **fewer** refer to numbers (things we can count).

Much and **less** refer to quantities or amounts.

So, for example:

He asked **many** questions. (refers to the *number* of questions he asked)

There are **fewer** children in the playground today. (refers to the *number* of children in the playground)

There was **much** excitement when they opened their presents. (a large *amount* of excitement)

It was **less** terrifying than he had imagined. (a smaller *amount* of fear)

Activity

Practise your use of these pairs by:

■ deciding whether the following items or people refer to a number or an amount;

■ placing the words in the correct column.

women; chickens; disappointment; drink; pencils; money; enjoyment; practice; houses; collections

number	*amount*
many:fewer	**much:less**

For the *number* column you should have chosen items which can be counted: women, chickens, pencils, houses, collections; the rest will need to be under the heading *amount*.

Review

In this unit we have covered a variety of common confusions. You should now be able to:

■ identify pairs of words that can cause confusion;

■ make the right choice of words to convey your meaning.

If you have made mistakes with any of these constructions in the past, you may find it difficult to break the habit. Always check your written work when you have completed it, making a special check for your confusions.

UNIT 6
BEING CONSISTENT

Targets

This unit will help you to:

→ ensure that verbs agree with their subjects;

→ use pronouns consistently in sentences;

→ use the correct subject/object pronouns in sentences.

Before you study this unit you may find it helpful to look back to the points about verbs and pronouns that you covered in Unit 2.

Subject and verb

The subject is the person or thing that does the action; the verb describes the action.

Verb forms may change according to whether the subject is singular or plural or whether the first, second or third person form is being used, for example:

singular				*plural*
I **was writing**.	←	1st person form	→	We **were writing**.
You **were writing**.	←	2nd person form	→	You **were writing**.
He/ she **was writing**.	←	3rd person form	→	They **were writing**.

When a verb has the correct form for its subject we say that the verb 'agrees' with its subject. Most of the time we are able to ensure such agreement spontaneously but occasionally we need to think about it more carefully.

Activity

See how much you already know about verb and subject agreements by completing each space in the passage below with either **was** or **were**.

The day of the competition finally arrived and everyone in the village _____ excited. By seven o'clock the villagers _____ waiting for the coach which _____ to take them to Winsham. The choir _____ due to sing in the Town Hall at 10.00 a.m. and no one _____ going to miss the performance.

(continued opposite)

> Every villager [   ] involved whether that meant helping with the costumes, carrying music stands or just being part of the audience.
>
> The choir, who [   ] all wearing different costumes, looked splendid as they filed on to the stage. They sang magnificently, although one of the singers [   ] out of tune.

Compare your choices with those shown below. (Ignore the inserted numbers for the moment.)

> The day of the competition finally arrived and everyone in the village **was**[1] excited. By seven o'clock the villagers **were**[2] waiting for the coach which **was**[3] to take them to Winsham. The choir **was**[4] due to sing in the Town Hall at 10.00 a.m. and no one **was**[5] going to miss the performance. Every villager **was**[6] involved whether that meant helping with the costumes, carrying music stands or just being part of the audience.
>
> The choir, who **were**[7] all wearing different costumes, looked splendid as they filed on to the stage. They sang magnificently, although one of the singers **was**[8] out of tune.

Did you:

■ always make the right choice in each one?

■ understand the reason for the correct choice?

If either of your answers to the questions above was 'No', you will find it helpful to study the suggestions below. The number after each point directs you back to the passage and shows you an example of that point in the passage.

Choosing the correct form

After a singular subject, for example, **I**, **it**, **he**, **she**, **Paul**, **Mr Smith**, choose a singular verb form, for example, **am**, **is** (present tense), **was** (past tense):

3 – the *coach* which **was** …

After a plural subject, for example, **we**, **they**, **the Smiths**, **the singers**, **horses**, choose a plural verb form, for example, **are** (present tense), **were** (past tense):

2 – the *villagers* **were** waiting …

When you use these words as the subject:

■ **everyone**;

■ **anyone**;

■ **someone**;

■ **no one**.

or these words with a subject word:

- **every** (e.g. every girl, every dog);

- **each** (e.g. each person, each day);

- **none** (e.g. none of the students, none of her work).

use a singular verb form:

1 – everyone in the village **was** excited

5 – no one **was** going to miss the performance

6 – every villager **was** involved.

Some subjects may appear at first to be plural but are in fact singular, so a singular verb form is used:

8 – one of the singers **was** out of tune. (The subject is 'one singer' not 'singers'.)

When a group of people, animals or things is treated as a single unit, the verb form is singular:

4 – The *choir* **was** due to sing … (The choir is made up of several singers but they are singing together as one unit.)

When the individuality of the group members is being stressed, the verb form is plural:

7 – the *choir,* **were** all wearing different costumes … (Their individuality is being stressed.)

By the way

The passage you've just been studying is written in the past tense. However, agreement between subject and verb is necessary whichever tense you are using.

Activity

The following passage contains examples of many of the points that you've practised so far in this unit. Read it through and look at the choices of verb forms. Then cross through the incorrect one in each case.

We **are/is** hoping to go to Paris this spring. Everyone we **know/knows** who **has/have** been there **tell/tells** us how wonderful Paris **is/are** in the springtime. We **is/are** going to fly from Bristol as there **is/are** a very good service which **leaves/leave** at nine o'clock. One of our friends **is/are** going to meet us at the airport in Paris. Our friend **has/have** lived in Paris for four years but now the company which **employs/employ** her **are/is** dismissing all the staff who **works/work** in Paris. Each member of staff **is/are** going to be offered the chance to move to London but none of them **is/are** very enthusiastic.

Now check your choices against those shown overleaf. If you found any of these difficult you will need to check back through the unit.

> We **are** hoping to go to Paris this spring. Everyone we **know** who **has** been there **tells** us how wonderful Paris **is** in the springtime. We **are** going to fly from Bristol as there **is** a very good service which **leaves** at nine o'clock. One of our friends **is** going to meet us at the airport in Paris. Our friend **has** lived in Paris for four years but now the company which **employs** her **is** dismissing all of the staff who **work** in Paris. Each member of staff **is** going to be offered the chance to move to London but none of them **is** very enthusiastic.

Pronouns

Male or female

In the previous section of this unit you saw that it is possible to become confused about whether to use a singular or plural verb form when you use these words:

<blockquote>every   each   anyone   someone   no one   everybody   everyone.</blockquote>

You will remember that when such words are used, the subject is singular, so you should use a singular verb form. Look at the following sentences:

---

1   **Each** of the girls brought **her** own dinner.

2   **Every** dog was sitting by **its** owner.

3   **Everyone** must hand in **their** homework.

4   **Someone** stole the money and I'm waiting for **him** or **her** to own up.

You will have seen that on most occasions we use a singular pronoun after such words as **everyone, someone** etc. In (1) and (2) the choice is easy to make, but in (3) and (4) it is more difficult.

What are the choices?

- ■ You could overcome the problem of choosing a pronoun by opting for **his** but you may feel that this is sexist.

- ■ You can use **his or her**, or **him or her** (as in Sentence 4), but this can become clumsy.

- ■ You may prefer to use **their** (as in Sentence 3) and deliberately ignore the rules for singular subjects, pronouns and verbs. In such instances the choice is yours. Few experts would insist that the rules should be always be followed.

Subjects and objects

Subject pronouns are: I, **you, he, she, it, we, they**.

Object pronouns are: **me, you, him, her, us, them**.

Activity

Study the following two pairs of sentences. Which sentence in each pair is correct?

Fatima and me are coming to stay next week.

Fatima and I are coming to stay next week.

Sheila invited Fatima and me to stay.

Sheila invited Fatima and I to stay.

In the past you may have been told that in such sentences it is correct to refer to yourself as **I**. You may even feel that it sounds better or more grammatical, but you would be correct to use **I** only in the first pair. In the second pair the correct pronoun to choose is **me**.

■ In the first pair 'Fatima and I' is the subject of the sentence so the subject pronoun **I** is chosen.

■ In the second pair 'Fatima and me' is the object of the sentence. Sheila is the subject. She is doing the inviting, whereas 'Fatima and me' are having the inviting done to us! The object pronoun **me** is chosen.

By the way

■ **You** and **it** stay the same whether they are used as the subject or the object of a verb.

■ Object pronouns are also used after a preposition, for example:

The cat leapt towards Robert and **me**. (preposition = towards)

■ If you are referring to yourself and another person, you should refer to the other person first, for example:

John and I went to see Jeff.

He gave it to Paul and me.

Review

Think about the targets for this unit. Do you feel that you understand more about agreement, and subject and object pronouns? There will probably still be times when you will have to think carefully about whether you have chosen the right verb form or the right pronoun. You can check agreement by remembering that:

■ A singular subject usually needs a singular verb and pronoun.

and you can choose the correct pronoun if:

■ You decide whether the pronoun is the subject or object of the verb.

UNIT 7

USING VERBS CORRECTLY

Targets

This unit will help you to:

→ recognise the way in which verbs are structured;

→ identify any points about verbs that you may need to practise;

→ use verbs correctly.

This unit covers those situations when you might be uncertain about the verb you have chosen. You will also be encouraged to read through your writing to check that you haven't mixed up tenses or used an incomplete verb. Before you set out on this unit you may like to look back to Unit 2 to remind yourself of the technical terms used in discussing verbs.

Activity

Each of the following sentences contains one of the errors that we will consider in this unit. As you read each of the sentences, see if you can note down a correct version in the box beneath.

1   The children talking with their parents.

2   He rung the bell.

3   I was running along the road when he drives past.

The corrected verbs are shown in the diagram below, together with a note of the sections of this unit which explain how to ensure you use the verb correctly.

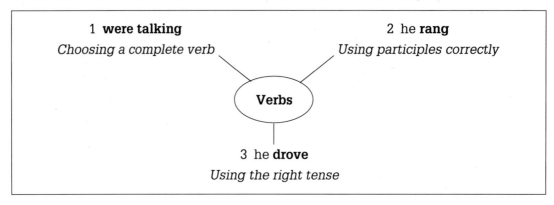

1 **were talking**
Choosing a complete verb

2 he **rang**
Using participles correctly

Verbs

3 he **drove**
Using the right tense

Choosing a complete verb

In Example 1:

> The children talking with their parents

you saw that we needed to add the auxiliary verb **were** for the verb to be correct and the sentence to make sense.

> The children **were talking** with their parents.

In Unit 2 we showed you that in certain tenses the complete verb is made up of a participle and an auxiliary verb. Without the auxiliary verb to complete it, we don't know when the action happened.

■   The auxiliary verb **were** shows us that the action happened in the past.

By the way

The auxiliary verbs we use to show time are formed from the verbs **to be** and **to have**:

■   I **am** eating.

■   I **have** eaten.

Activity

> Which of the following sentences contain incomplete verbs?
>
> 1   Lucy was choosing a new handbag when her purse was stolen.
>
> 2   The government hoping for inflation to fall.
>
> 3   The contents of the filing cabinet strewn everywhere.
>
> 4   I hope that you coming tonight.
>
> 5   The children running and jumping.

Numbers 2 to 5 contain incomplete verbs: hoping, strewn, coming, running. Each of the verbs needs an auxiliary verb to complete it: is hoping; had been strewn; are coming; were running.

Activity

> In the passage below some verbs need to be completed in order to make sense. Try rewriting the passage. (Use a separate sheet for this.)
>
> > Peter loitering outside the door. He was trying to pluck up courage to go into the noisy room. Inside, other people dancing, drinking and enjoying themselves but he felt too awkward to join them. It began to rain. Soon, water from a leaking gutter pouring down on him. His clothes soaked and he was just about to walk away when the door opened. Light and warmth streamed out and deciding that after all he had nothing to lose, he crept in.

We have highlighted the auxiliary verbs that we've added. Your choices should be the same.

> Peter **was** loitering outside the door. He was trying to pluck up courage to go into the noisy room. Inside, other people **were** dancing, drinking and enjoying themselves but he felt too awkward to join them. It began to rain. Soon, water from a leaking gutter **was** pouring down on him. His clothes **were** soaked and he was just about to walk away when the door opened. Light and warmth streamed out and deciding that after all he had nothing to lose, he crept in.

Using participles correctly

Is it correct to say:

- He drunk the wine;

  or

- He drank the wine?

Drank is the correct verb to use on this occasion. **Drunk** is a past participle.

You will have seen in the previous section that a participle needs an auxiliary verb to form a complete verb:

He **had drunk** the wine.   He **had rung** the bell.

are now correct.

You may sometimes feel uncertain about verbs like **rang** and **rung** and **drank** and **drunk** because the two verbs within each pair have a similar sound and it is easy to make the wrong choice.

Activity

Check that you can make the right choice between these verbs:

1   She sung/sang an aria from *Figaro*.

2   The performance had already begun/began when I entered.

3   The drains stunk/stank so much we felt quite sick.

4   The water was froze/frozen this morning

5   I did/done my best in the competition but I was beat/beaten by Jess.

You should have chosen these verbs: sang; begun; stank; frozen; did and beaten. You will notice that where you chose the past participle of the verb (begun, frozen, beaten) there was an auxiliary verb to complete the construction: had begun; was frozen; was beaten.

Most past participles end in **ed** or **en** (e.g. **washed** and **broken**) but some are irregular. You have already encountered **rung, drunk, sung, begun, stunk, done** – all of which are irregular. Some other irregular past participles keep the same spelling as the verb in the past simple tense:

Yesterday he **hurt** his ankle. (past simple tense)

Having **hurt** his ankle, he was unable to play golf. (past participle)

With other verbs the past participle is entirely different:

They **went** for a walk this morning. (past simple tense)

When I called for them, I was told they had **gone** for a walk. (past participle)

Activity

Complete this passage by constructing the past participles of the verbs shown inside the brackets. Use a separate sheet for this.

I knew that I was (mistake) as soon as she started to speak. I thought that I had (know) her at work but, as soon as I heard her Scottish accent, I realised that I had (chose) the wrong person. When she had (go), I looked around the room again. I had just (catch) sight of someone else who might have been Sheila when a hand was (place) on my shoulder and I heard an unmistakable voice whisper in my ear, 'Gotcha!'

The participles are: mistaken, known, chosen, gone, caught, placed.

By the way

When you read through your writing you can check whether you have used participles correctly by:

■   looking to see that you've included an appropriate auxiliary verb;

■   checking in your dictionary that you've chosen the correct construction for the past participle. Most good concise dictionaries will list the past tense and past participles under the verb, for example:

swim *v.* (past tense *swam* past part. *swum*).

Using the right tense

In Sentence 3 in the activity on page 41, we have mixed up the tenses. The first verb is in the past tense but the second verb is in the present tense:

I **was running** along the road when he **drives** past.

In this sentence this mixture of tenses is incorrect. Both actions must happen either in the present or in the past:

I **am running** along the road when he **drives past**. (present tense)

I **was running** along the road when he **drove past**. (past tense)

However, sometimes you will quite rightly need to change from one tense to another:

I **am** certain that he **died** several years ago.

present tense   past tense

You should now be more aware of tenses, so that when you read through a completed piece of writing you can check that any changes in tense you've made are necessary.

Activity

Check this piece of writing to see whether the tenses have been unnecessarily mixed and make any corrections that you feel are necessary.

On Lap 2 Mansell goes very fast and beat the lap record but later he slowed down and lets the other drivers overtake him. After refuelling he picks up speed and fought his way to the Number One position. At one time Mansell and Senna were driving side by side and neither is willing to give way. Eventually Mansell overtakes and remains in front until the end.

You probably decided that this passage would be best in the past tense and so made these corrections: went very fast; let the other drivers overtake; picked up speed: neither was willing; Mansell overtook and remained in front.

Review

Look back to the targets for this unit and check whether you feel you have attained them. You should now feel more confident about using verbs correctly and be more aware of when you have made a mistake so that you can correct it. You might also find it helpful in the next few days to pay particular attention to the way other people use verbs. See if you can spot any examples of the mistakes we've outlined in this unit!

UNIT 8 — REVIEWING YOUR PROGRESS

Targets

This unit will help you to:

➔ review what you have achieved;

➔ identify the areas you still need to work on;

➔ decide where you go from here.

What have you achieved?

As you have worked through this book, you may have encountered points which were new to you, or revised grammatical constructions that you once knew but which had become a little hazy in your mind.

Activity

When you have reached the end of a period of study, it is useful to consider what you have gained. We suggest you set aside five to ten minutes to make a list of the points that you have learnt or revised and the areas you now feel confident about. Use a separate sheet of paper for this.

What do you need to work on?

Now review what you have written in response to the last activity. Possibly there are some aspects of the book that you would like to look at again. It would be helpful to have a record of these, too, so that you can concentrate on them in the future.

Activity

In order to draw up a list of the points you still need to practise, go back through the units. Look particularly at the targets and headings, which will help to remind you of the contents of each unit. Make a note of the things you still need to work on.

Where next?

In this section we consider three options that are now open to you. Bear in mind that none of these excludes the other two.

More practice

Do as much formal writing as possible so that you can put your grammar into practice. Most of us have some bad grammatical habits and it is only by repeatedly practising the correct constructions that we will remember them and replace our bad habits with good practice. Now that you have completed this book you are aware of many of the grammatical pitfalls and understand the correct constructions to use.

A checking routine

We have already drawn your attention to the importance of checking your written work. By developing a routine for this you will more readily be able to detect your mistakes.

Of course, if you are completing a timed assignment or taking an exam, checking time is limited, but you still need to organise your time so that at least 5 – 10 minutes can be devoted to checking. When you are doing written work at home, you can more easily concentrate on the checking process.

What do you need to look for when you are checking?

Your own bad habits

By now you will know the types of mistake you are likely to make. At the beginning of this unit you made a list of the areas you felt you still needed to work on, so look out particularly for these.

Common errors

This book has concentrated on mistakes which people frequently make, in both speech and writing. Here is a list of the main points we have covered, which you can use as a checklist when you read through your work.

Grammar checklist

Things to avoid:
- colloquial words and expressions
- over-worked similes
- tautology
- slang
- double negatives
- ambiguous words and phrases.

Things to ensure you use correctly:

verbs
- agreement with subject
- using a complete verb
- using the correct past participle
- knowing which verb to choose from
- confusing pairs e.g. lay: lie
- maintaining the correct tense

pronouns
- subject or object?
- singular or plural?

Checking may at first seem a lengthy and laborious process, but as you become accustomed to your routine you will find you can check more quickly and thoroughly. Eventually you will be able to dispense with the checklist.

Developing style

Each of us has a different style of writing. We could each write about the same subject and include the same main points, but the ways in which we expressed ourselves would be different.

When you make a thorough check of your work, look at the construction of each sentence individually. By working on individual sentences you will be considering your style of writing. Your message should be concise and unambiguous.

At times you may not notice any obvious grammatical mistakes in a sentence but you may feel that the sentence doesn't sound quite right. It is very difficult to explain what is meant by 'sound right', but we are sure you will have had the experience of feeling uneasy about the style of something you have written or heard yourself say. If this is ever the case, always ask yourself if the sentence would be better expressed in a slightly different way. For example:

> During my first week of training, I feel I gained confidence.

Does the version below sound better?

> I feel I gained confidence during my first week of training.

Your aim should be to develop a personal but effective style of writing. You may find other learners or colleagues who are willing to lend you their reports, letters, essays or assignments so that you can look at the way they express themselves. Wide reading will also allow you to consider different styles of writing. You can then compare these with your own. In all this, remember that your style of writing is not fixed forever: you can change and improve it with help from others if you want to.

Review

We hope that you have enjoyed this book and that it has made you reflect on the importance of correct grammar.

You may enjoy putting your grammatical achievements into practice by doing a piece of writing. The choice of subject is entirely up to you. We would only advise you to choose a subject that you can write about freely and which requires a formal style. When you have completed it, check it very carefully, paying particular attention to your areas of weakness, then use the checklist on page 47.

If you have a tutor, ask him or her to look at your writing and point out any grammatical errors. It would also be helpful if he or she could comment upon your style of writing.

Good luck! We hope you will use your grammar to good effect.

GRAMMAR

ASSIGNMENTS FOR TUTORIAL COMMENT

NATIONAL
EXTENSION
COLLEGE

Introduction

These assignments are intended for learners studying with an NEC tutor. Each of the assignments should be carried out at the point indicated. You should send an assignment to your tutor as soon as you have completed all its parts. Your tutor will mark your answers and give you personal help. He or she will also deal with any difficulties you meet, and help you to adapt the course to suit your own circumstances.

Treat each assignment as a further step to learning. Don't worry about making mistakes; the word 'error' originally meant 'wandering about looking for something'. It is through making errors that we learn things and find what it is that we are looking for. However, if you feel unsure of how to respond to a question, write to your tutor and ask for advice. While you are waiting for a reply, go on to the next Unit.

Bear in mind the contribution that your family and friends can make to your learning. Discuss ideas with them and if possible persuade them to read your assignments and comment on them before you send them to your tutor.

How to present your assignments

Please follow these instructions for all your assignments.

1 Leave a margin of one and a half inches (about 4cm) on the left side of the page and three inches (about 8cm) along the bottom. This space is for your tutor's comments.

2 If you are not typing your assignments, make sure that your handwriting is clear. Use pen not pencil.

3 Number each question clearly.

ASSIGNMENT A

Send this to your tutor when you have completed Unit 1

For your first assignment we would like you to send to your tutor a short letter giving some background details of yourself and your aims.

- Begin your letter by writing down some brief details about your current studies or work – paid or unpaid.

- Then write a few words about what you hope to gain from the course and why good grammar is important to you. We ask you to consider this point in the activity on page 7 of Unit 1. Following the activity we suggested some possible reasons, but our list is not exhaustive and you may well have other suggestions.

- Finally, tell your tutor which grammar points you feel you particularly need to work on. Pages 8 to 10 of Unit 1 will help you to decide this.

ASSIGNMENT B

Send this to your tutor when you have completed Unit 2

Unit 2 has provided you with a great deal of background information. You are unlikely to have all this at your fingertips yet. Instead we would expect you to refer to the unit from time to time as you work through the rest of the course. However, it is important to ensure that at this point you understand the basic concepts we have discussed. The two parts of this assignment aim to help you in this.

Part 1

For the first part of this assignment we would like you to identify some of the parts of speech in the following passage. Study the passage carefully and then follow the instructions at the top of the next page.

> Later that day they set sail for the island. Their hosts had warned them of treacherous currents in the narrow channel between North Point and the harbour, but their ketch ploughed steadily through the moderate swell. When they landed, a small group of islanders was waiting anxiously to meet them. At their head stood the president of the island council. 'Welcome to Netherholm,' he announced. 'This is indeed an important occasion.' Having said this he led them up the steep lane towards the prison.

Now see if you can select from the passage and note down for your tutor:

- two pronouns   • one auxiliary verb   • two adverbs   • three adjectives
- one irregular verb   • three nouns   • one verb in the infinitive.

Part 2

Finally, send to your tutor a note of any queries that you have as a result of your work on Unit 2.

ASSIGNMENT C

Send this to your tutor when you have completed Unit 4.

Part 1

Complete this part when you reach the end of Unit 3.

The following passage contains one or more examples of each of the four pitfalls that we introduced in Unit 3:

- colloquialisms

- overworked similes

- tautology

- slang.

Your task is to rewrite the passage, eliminating these features. Bear in mind that there is no single right way of doing this. You may can be as you creative as you wish, provided the sense remains the same.

> I was sitting on my backside, happy as a sandboy, when this old geezer came up to me on a bike. He said that chucking old booze cans down the mineshaft was needless waste, and that there was a place where cans could be recycled again, across the common in Amelia Street. I told him where to go in no uncertain terms. He went as red as a beetroot and scooted off, saying that he was going to tell the fuzz. I was rattled, I can tell you. But that's all past history now. I've put a final end to that sort of behaviour and this year I'm entering for the 'Evening News' Green Teen award.

Part 2

Complete this part when you reach the end of Unit 4

Unit 4 aims to help you write more precisely. The following passage contains examples of some of the problems addressed in the unit. These are:

• double negatives   • sentence order   • confusing pronouns.

See if you can rewrite the passage in a way that eliminates these. At some points you may need to make assumptions about the intended meaning.

Jan didn't eat all morning. He was worried that Les hadn't told no one about the attack. In the afternoon he wrote a note to the shopkeeper with a shaky hand. In the evening the shopkeeper replied, asking him to write an account of the incident with his name at the top. He said burglars had injured his wife, not Jan and Les, and that they hadn't taken no part in the incident.

When you have completed your rewrite of the passage send it to your tutor, together with your work on Part 1. Add a brief note of any queries you have as a result of your work on Units 3 and 4.

ASSIGNMENT D

Send this to your tutor when you have completed Unit 6.

Part 1

Complete this when you reach the end of Unit 5.

(a) Unit 5 gives you help in choosing the correct verb from pairs that are easily confused. See if you can choose the right verb in each of the following sentences. Is it 'lie' or is it 'lay'? (Write out each sentence for your tutor.)

Yesterday we ___ on the lawn reading all afternoon.

The Swan had ___ three eggs in March.

James has ___ in the bath for half an hour.

I'll make Sue a cup of tea before she ___ the flooring.

You may believe him but I think he's ___ .

Don't ___ your washing on the wet paint!

(b) While you are studying Unit 6, listen to other people and collect examples of verbs being misused. Send your tutor a note of these when you have completed the unit.

Part 2

Complete this when you reach the end of Unit 6

Unit 6 stresses the importance of consistency, focusing on the use of verbs and pronouns. Part 2 of this assignment gives you the chance to practise this and obtain feedback from your tutor on your progress.

Write out the following passage, completing the gaps. All the missing words are either verbs or pronouns.

> Everyone ___ there for the concert. Bella and ___ arrived early but Dan was late. He said that someone had rung ___ as he was about to leave. People who come to the monthly concert ___ usually in their twenties but those who ___ older always find something to enjoy. It's a great way to spend an evening. Ask any of the guests who ___ regularly what attracts ___. They'll all ___ the same thing: 'Atmosphere!'

Don't forget to send both parts of this assignment to your tutor when you have completed Part 2, together with a note of any queries arising from your studies.

ASSIGNMENT E

Send this to your tutor when you have completed Unit 8

Unit 7 helps you to practise using verbs correctly. The first part of this assignment gives you the chance to apply your learning to some further examples.

Part 1

Tackle this when you reach the end of Unit 7

(a) Complete the following sentences (write them out for your tutor):

Many people ___ hoping for a change of government.

Posters ___ put up by the bus stop.

Here's John. I see he ___ walking with a limp.

(b) Write out the following sentences choosing the correct word in each case:

Someone had rung/rang for the ambulance.

Ford was chose/chosen for the star role.

The bird had flown/flied straight at the window.

He drew/drawn a picture of a mouse.

(c) Rewrite the following passage, changing the report from the present to the past tense; ie begin it with 'I was walking...':

> I am walking home one evening when an ancient black car pulls up beside me. The driver winds the window down and asks me if I can tell him the way to Crimples Farmhouse. I say I have never heard of anywhere by that name and suggest that he tries at the pub. The next day I ask at the Black Horse and they say that no one called last night but that there used to be a Crimples Farmhouse on the Hoathley road. It burnt down fifty years ago.

Part 2

Read this before you begin work on Unit 8

(a) On page 46 of Unit 8 we ask you to consider your overall progress during this course. For the second part of this assignment we would like you to send to your tutor your responses to the questions that we ask:

- What have you achieved?

- What aspects of grammar do you need to work on?

- What do you plan to do next?

Aim to write about one side in answer to the three questions.

(b) At the end of Unit 8 we suggest you carry out a short piece of writing. You should forward this to your tutor for comment with the other work you have carried out for this assignment. Your choice of topic is entirely up to you, but you should aim for between 300 and 500 words in total.

Don't forget to:

- check your writing before you send it off

- send your work on Parts 1 and 2 of this assignment to your tutor for comment.